The Farewell Symphony

Anna Harwell Celenza

Illustrated by JoAnn E. Kitchel

Charlesbridge

2005 First paperback edition
Text copyright © 2000 by Anna Harwell Celenza
Illustrations copyright © 2000 by JoAnn E. Kitchel

Published by Charlesbridge
85 Main Street, Watertown, MA 02472
(617) 926-0329
www.charlesbridge.com

Library of Congress Cataloging-in-Publication Data
Celenza, Anna Harwell.
The farewell symphony/Anna Harwell Celenza; illustrated by JoAnn E. Kitchel.
p.   cm.
Summary: In 1772, with summer long gone and winter fast approaching, Joseph Haydn,
court musician to Prince Nicholas of Esterházy, creates a symphony that finally persuades his
oblivious employer to close up his summer palace and allow the staff to return home.
ISBN 1-57091-406-0 (reinforced for library use)
ISBN 1-57091-407-9 (softcover)
1. Haydn, Joseph, 1732-1809—Juvenile fiction. [1. Haydn, Joseph, 1732-1809—Fiction.
2. Composers—Fiction.] I. Kitchel, JoAnn E., ill. II. Haydn, Joseph, 1732-1809.
Symphonies, H. I, 45, F# minor. III. Title.
PZ7.C314   Far 2000
[E]—dc21   99-047970

Printed in Korea
(hc) 10 9 8 7 6 5 4 3
(sc) 10 9 8 7 6 5 4 3 2 1

Illustrations done in watercolor and ink on Arches cold press paper
Display type and text type set in Giovanni and Della Robbia
Color separations by Sung In Printing, South Korea
Printed and bound by Sung In Printing, South Korea
Production supervision by Brian G. Walker
Designed by Diane M. Earley

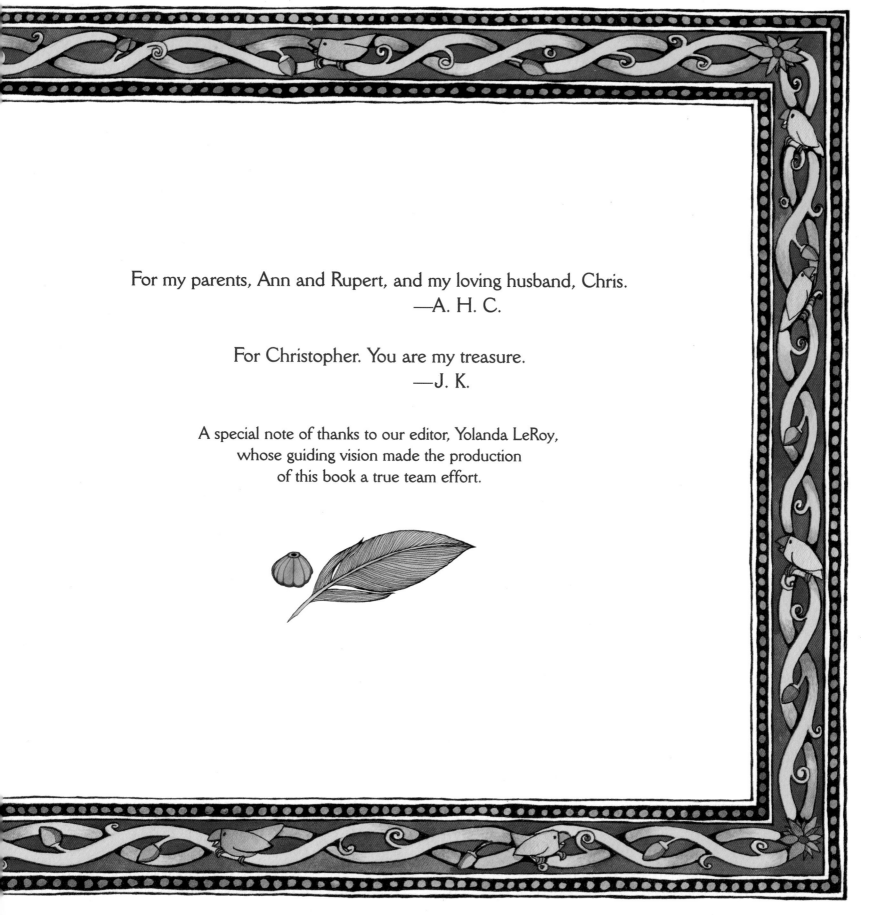

For my parents, Ann and Rupert, and my loving husband, Chris.
—A. H. C.

For Christopher. You are my treasure.
—J. K.

A special note of thanks to our editor, Yolanda LeRoy,
whose guiding vision made the production
of this book a true team effort.

 here are my trunks of clothes?" bellowed Prince Nicholas. "And my chess set and the silver candlesticks?"

"They are all on the wagons, sir," replied a weary servant.

"Haydn!" the prince shouted. "Are the instruments packed? What about the musicians? Where are all the musicians?"

"They are saying farewell to their families, sir," Haydn replied.

"Well, tell them to hurry up!" barked the prince. "I am ready to leave."

This was the scene at Prince Nicholas's winter estate in Eisenstadt, Austria, on a sunny March morning in 1772. The winter's snow had just started to melt, and Prince Nicholas was preparing for the annual move to his summer palace in the Hungarian countryside. The palace was called Esterháza, and it was the prince's pride and joy.

Accompanying the prince were twenty-two musicians and the royal music director, Joseph Haydn. Haydn was an excellent composer, famous throughout Europe. He wrote music for Prince Nicholas, but that was not his only responsibility. He also made sure that the musicians practiced diligently and stayed out of trouble. Haydn was even in charge of repairing broken instruments.

The musicians had many duties themselves. They were hired to keep Prince Nicholas and his many guests entertained. This was by no means an easy task. Prince Nicholas could never have enough musical entertainment. He demanded opera and ballet in the evenings, chamber music in the afternoons, outdoor music for strolls in the garden, dance music at formal balls, dinner music with special meals, heralding trumpeters for the arrival of guests, and sacred music for the palace chapel.

In short, Haydn and the musicians were kept very busy at Esterháza—so busy that they hardly missed their wives and children during the first few weeks. As summer wore on, though, homesickness set in, and the musicians began to complain. Toward the end of July the first violinist, Tomasini, came to Haydn and pleaded, "Papa Haydn, will you please go to Prince Nicholas and request that our families be allowed to join us? We are working very hard to please His Majesty, and it would comfort us so if our wives and children were here."

The next day Haydn went to the prince. "Your Highness," he cautiously began, "the musicians have asked me to speak to you. They are all quite homesick, and they miss their families. Please, sir, will you give them permission to invite their loved ones to Esterháza?"

"*What?*" the prince roared. "They want to invite their families? Never have I heard such impertinence. Who do the musicians think they are? The palace only has one hundred and twenty-six rooms. With all my important guests, there is not enough room for each servant's family. Haydn, you tell your musicians that if they want to keep their jobs, they will learn to live without their families for a while."

A dejected Haydn returned to his quarters. The musicians were waiting for him. "What did he say?" they asked. "When can we send for our families?"

"Never," Haydn glumly replied. "The prince will not allow it."

"*What?*" the musicians roared.

"Never have I known such cruelty!" shouted Tomasini. "We should march over to the palace and let Prince Nicholas know how angry we are."

"Yes!" cried the others. "We should tell the prince just how we feel."

"No. Listen to me, please," Haydn interrupted. "Going to Prince Nicholas will only make matters worse. He has threatened to fire those who complain again. Living without your families might be difficult, but living without your wages would be impossible. Please, gentlemen, do not make trouble. The end of summer is only a few weeks away. Before you know it, we will all be home again."

"Papa Haydn is right," Tomasini admitted. "We cannot fight the prince. We should get back to work and wait for the end of summer."

And so they did. Week after week passed, but Prince Nicholas never announced it was time to leave. The days grew shorter, a chill crept into the air, the leaves changed color, and still the prince never talked about going home.

The musicians grew restless. In November, Tomasini approached Haydn in a state of panic. "Papa Haydn," he cried, "why is the prince keeping us here so long? Please, go to him and convince him it is time to go home."

But Haydn was cautious. He remembered how the prince had reacted the last time the musicians made a request. "It will take a great deal of cleverness and tact to influence the prince," Haydn thought to himself. He turned to Tomasini and said, "Tell all the musicians to be patient and continue their duties as usual. I will think of something."

Haydn went for a walk in the garden and tried to think of a plan. He retired to his room and paced up and down. "Think! Think!" he muttered to himself. But no matter how hard he tried, Haydn could not find a solution. Frustrated, he sat down at his harpsichord and began working on a new composition to take his mind off his troubles.

All at once it came to him—the perfect plan. Haydn quickly pulled out a fresh piece of paper and feverishly began working on a new symphony. Less than two weeks later he presented the finished symphony to his musicians. "Study your parts carefully," he warned. "We must give our best performance. The prince has kept us here far too long, and if this symphony has the effect I think it will, we should all be home by the end of the month."

"Hooray!" the musicians cheered. They set to work learning their parts.

On the night of the performance the orchestra was already onstage when Prince Nicholas and his guests entered the candlelit theater. "Good evening, Haydn," said the prince. "I hope you have something special for me tonight."

"Oh, very special, indeed," Haydn answered. "We shall perform a new work, my Symphony in F-sharp minor."

"F-sharp minor?" the prince asked. "Is that not a rather unusual key?"

"Why, yes, it is," Haydn responded. "As you are about to hear, this is a rather unusual symphony. The emotions of my fellow musicians inspired the music. We hope that you will find our performance enlightening."

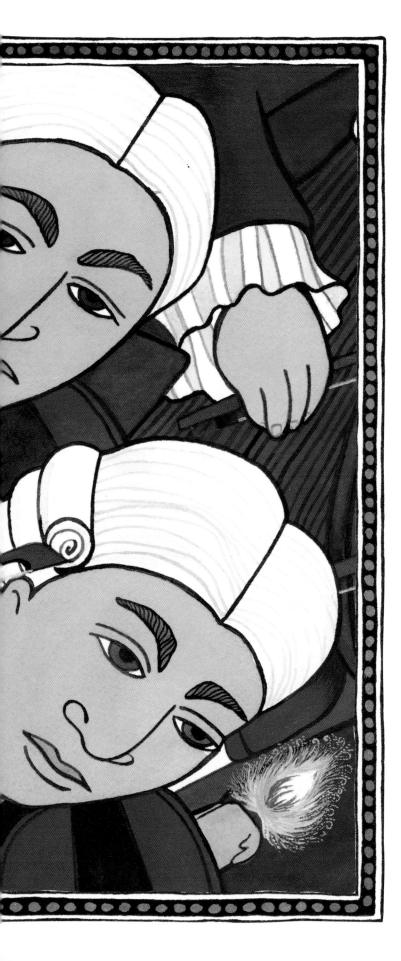

A quizzical look passed over Prince Nicholas's face as Haydn took his place onstage and picked up his violin. The hall was in total silence. All the musicians looked to Haydn for their cue. He gave a slight nod of his head, and a rush of music burst forth from the strings and swooped down from the stage. Explosive chords merged with surging melodies as streams of quick, repetitive notes enclosed the audience in a whirlpool of tension. Prince Nicholas grasped the arms of his chair. "This is angry music!" he thought. For the first time, the prince was feeling the musicians' frustration over having to remain at Esterháza.

The second movement began quite differently. The notes did not rush forward as they had in the first movement. Instead, light splashes of sound trickled from the violins. The violas and cellos joined in. A sorrowful tune rose from the stage and passed from one instrument to the next, first to a violin and then to an oboe. A tear rolled down the prince's cheek. "This music is beautiful and yet so sad," he thought. For the first time, the prince was feeling the musicians' sorrow over being separated from their families.

When the third movement began, Prince Nicholas smiled. He could hear at once that it was based on a dance called the minuet. "How graceful," he thought as the violins played the opening notes. Just then the horns and cellos broke in: *"Blaaaap!"*

At first the prince thought they had made a mistake. "Those stupid musicians played a wrong note," he grumbled. But then the orchestra repeated the passage, and it happened again! The prince frowned. He remembered all the dances that had taken place at Esterháza that summer. Prince Nicholas loved to dance, but he knew in his heart he was a terrible dancer—always stumbling and stomping on the ladies' toes. The prince scowled at the orchestra. "They are mocking me!" he thought. For the first time, the prince was feeling the musicians' contempt for being treated so cruelly.

By the end of the third movement Prince Nicholas was thinking, "I have had quite enough of this new symphony." But then the fourth movement began—and it was magnificent! Every instrument strained with sound as waves of glorious music washed over the audience. The prince was fully enjoying the music when, suddenly, the orchestra stopped. After a brief pause the musicians began playing a slow, melancholy tune.

"What is this?" thought the prince. He leaned forward and eyed the orchestra carefully. Quite unexpectedly, two performers—an oboist and a horn player—stood up, closed their music, snuffed out their candles, and left the stage.

The prince was shocked. "What in the world is happening?" he thought. He was just about to say something when the bassoon player stood up and did the same thing. A few seconds later a second oboist left. A horn player followed, then the string bass player, and then the cellist. One by one each musician left the stage. In the end only Haydn and Tomasini remained, playing a slow, haunting duet. Then, like all the others, they stood up, closed their music, snuffed out their candles, and left the stage.

An awkward hush fell over the audience. The musicians waited anxiously backstage. Haydn peered nervously from behind the curtain into the darkened theater.

The prince sat motionless in his chair. He stared at the empty stage and thought about the music he had just experienced. Then he lifted his hands and slowly began to clap. "Bravo, Haydn!" bellowed the prince. "You have made your point. I realize now that I have kept the musicians here far too long. Summer has passed, and their families are waiting. Go to your rooms, everyone, and pack your bags. Tomorrow we head for home. Farewell, musicians. Farewell, Haydn. Farewell, Esterháza!"

The Eighteenth-Century Symphony

A symphony is a long piece of music played by an orchestra. Symphonies composed in the second half of the eighteenth century (the Classical period) generally contained four movements: an opening allegro, or fast movement; a lyrical slow movement; a dancelike movement called a minuet; and a brisk finale. Haydn followed this plan when he composed his Symphony No. 45 in F-sharp minor. He made one exception: At the end of the brisk finale he added a slow section—the famous "farewell" that convinced the prince to go home.

Today symphonies are often performed under the guidance of a conductor. In Haydn's day the members of the orchestra looked to one of the instrumentalists for their cue. Conductors were used only in complicated performances, such as operas, that included both singers and instrumentalists.

bassoon

horn

oboe

Haydn composed for what today would be called a chamber orchestra. The typical eighteenth-century orchestra consisted of seventeen to nineteen musicians. The instruments were divided into two categories: the string instruments and the wind instruments. Occasionally a keyboard instrument called a harpsichord was used as well.

The string instruments often included eight to ten violins, two violas, a cello, and a bass. The string instruments of the eighteenth century were very similar to the instruments played today.

The wind instruments often included two oboes, two horns, and a bassoon. These instruments were quite different from modern wind instruments. The oboes and bassoons had fewer keys, and the horns had no valves and were very difficult to play.

cello

viola

violin

bass

Author's Note

    The Farewell Symphony is a true story. The events in this book are based on documented evidence, and the characters—Prince Nicholas, Haydn, Tomasini, and the other musicians—really did exist.

    Franz Joseph Haydn (1732-1809) spent nearly thirty years working for Prince Nicholas of Esterházy (1714-1790). Documents from that period, now held in the Esterházy archives and various European libraries, reveal the composer's many activities at court. Haydn composed music as requested by the prince and was responsible for the care of all music and instruments. Haydn's contract, dated 1765, required him to behave and dress as an officer in a princely court and to serve as an example to the other musicians. The composer was a kind music director, and he soon earned the nickname "Papa Haydn."

    Archival documents from 1772 reveal various events that have been included in *The Farewell Symphony*. Descriptions are given of outdoor festivities, masked balls, special theatrical performances, concerts, elaborate ballet and opera productions, and the arrival of guests. Even the repair of musical instruments is documented. A pay sheet from 1772 lists twenty-three musicians (including Haydn and several singers), and a list written in Haydn's own hand keeps track of his many compositions. Haydn's letters to the prince reflect his role as a spokesman for the musicians. In one message, dated 1772, Haydn wrote: "I have communicated today to all the musicians by word of mouth your high order . . . that none of the wives and children of the musicians . . . are allowed to be seen at Esterháza. There was no one who did not agree to the terms of that high order."

    The first performance of Haydn's Symphony No. 45 in F-sharp minor was probably quite similar to the performance described in this book. The original music (now in Budapest) indicates when each musician is to stop playing and leave the room. Records also show that Prince Nicholas and his musicians left Esterháza shortly after the symphony's premiere.

    History rarely preserves the personal details that bring a story to life. Consequently, the personalities and emotions of the characters have been enhanced by my imagination. Also, the interpretation of the symphony, as experienced by Prince Nicholas, is based on my personal response to the music.